6/56/40

4.50

Mary Jane Anaway
'56

D1201927

June 30th, 1956
Our tenth –
Love from
Buz

MORRIS GRAVES

♦

MORRIS GRAVES

FREDERICK S. WIGHT

JOHN I. H. BAUR

DUNCAN PHILLIPS

UNIVERSITY OF CALIFORNIA PRESS

BERKELEY AND LOS ANGELES 1956

Uɴɪᴠᴇʀsɪᴛʏ ᴏꜰ Cᴀʟɪꜰᴏʀɴɪᴀ Pʀᴇss
Berkeley and Los Angeles, California

Cᴀᴍʙʀɪᴅɢᴇ Uɴɪᴠᴇʀsɪᴛʏ Pʀᴇss
London, England

Copyright, 1956, by The Regents of the University of California

Printed in the United States of America
By the University of California Printing Department

Library of Congress Catalog Card No.: 56–6990

Published for the Art Galleries, University of California, Los Angeles

Designed by Adrian Wilson

Second Printing

The occasion responsible for the publication of this book is the Morris Graves Retrospective Exhibition, organized by the Art Galleries of the University of California, Los Angeles, and shown in 1956 at the following participating institutions: Whitney Museum of American Art, New York; Phillips Gallery, Washington, D.C.; Museum of Fine Arts, Boston; Des Moines Art Center; M. H. de Young Memorial Museum, San Francisco; Art Galleries, University of California, Los Angeles; Art Center in La Jolla, California; and Seattle Art Museum.

The editor wishes to thank Kenneth Rexroth for permission to quote from his article, "The Visionary Painting of Morris Graves," in *Perspectives USA* (Number 10, Winter 1955); and Kenneth H. Roberts for making his bibliography available.

Perspectives USA has contributed the color plate: LITTLE-KNOWN BIRD OF THE INNER EYE, GUARDIAN, and INDIVIDUAL STATE OF THE WORLD; *Mademoiselle:* JOYOUS YOUNG PINE; *Vogue:* FISH REFLECTED UPON OUTER AND MENTAL SPACE and SPIRIT BIRD TRANSPORTING MINNOW FROM STREAM TO STREAM. The *Vogue* plates (copyright 1945, 1954) are used by permission of the Condé Nast Publications Inc.

Credit is due for use of the following photographs: SURF BIRDS, 1940, Detroit Institute of Arts; SEA AND THE MORNING REDNESS, Art Institute of Chicago; EAGLE IN THE ROCK, Dearborn-Massar, Seattle; DOVE OF THE INNER EYE and FRENCH NIGHTFALL PIECE, Museum of Modern Art, New York; JOURNEY, Whitney Museum of American Art, New York.

MORRIS GRAVES, *a photograph by Imogen Cunningham*

CONTENTS

JOURNEY, NO. 2, 1943
The Whitney Museum of American Art, New York

FOREWORD

Perhaps one reason that the paintings of Morris Graves pursue the imagination so persistently is that they seem to be riddles without answers, symbols with lost meanings, artifacts from a vanished age. They look like rubbings of prehistoric fossils or palimpsests beneath whose abraded surfaces some clue to significance lurks in tantalizing fragments. The wrinkled rice paper is like ancient silk or papyrus, the tarnished gold gleams fitfully, as if miraculously preserved from time, the stained colors and incrusted surfaces suggest an unexpected archaeological find. The quality of the drawing itself gives these images a look of something intended to communicate, as if they were the instruments of an old and sophisticated cult without a Rosetta Stone to unravel their original function.

We can, of course, find meanings, or at least moods, in much of Graves's work. From joyous pines at one pole to blind and wounded birds at another, a range of emotion is implicit. And, in some of his recent paintings especially, there are aesthetic meanings which seem fairly obvious—a decorative quality that is allied with Oriental art, a line that is both ritualistic and supremely sensitive in capturing the character of bird and fish. Yet these alone, though great accomplishments, do not explain the obsessive quality that lies at the heart of Graves's best work. To define this, one returns (with a sense that it is still an inadequate explanation) to the feeling of lost symbols from another age. Perhaps it is not so much another age as another spiritual level, remote from the climate of our average lives, so veiled, withdrawn, and intangible that it dissolves when one attempts to grasp it yet continues to captivate the mind with its pervasive and untimely presence.

JOHN I. H. BAUR

CHALICE, *ca.* 1942
The Phillips Gallery, Washington, D.C.

ABOUT THE TECHNIC

A word about the technic of Graves. One feels a solicitude for the survival of these rare visionary perceptions, committed, in gouache of tonal subtleties, to the thinnest of tissue paper. But this too is as it had to be. In no other medium and in no other way could this artist have expressed what he had to say about the insecurity and brevity of life and the poignant loveliness that can stir us for a second but may never return. He is seldom if ever literary—not even in the supernatural black and white of his CHALICE. What Morris Graves has to tell is almost invariably of what he has seen. His moody drawing and design, his fine placements in deep space without ever breaking through the picture plane are technical distinctions we recognize in a language worthy of comparison with great Chinese nature painting. But Graves is more than the virtuoso of a most delicate instrument. Graves is a mystic touched with genius, one who paints for "the inner eye." He haunts the mind and the senses like night sounds in a great stillness.

DUNCAN PHILLIPS

WOUNDED SCOTER, No. 2, 1944
The Cleveland Museum of Art. Gift of Gamblers in Modern Art.

MORRIS GRAVES

ON MEETING

Morris Graves is more poet than architect, which sets him apart from most of the painters of his time. He inflicts a difficult standard upon himself, for the work of the builders has only to stand up, but Graves's art must create a world remote from the world of gravity; the builders extend the living process, but Graves illuminates it. The objects he draws are not birds, but the bird after it nests in the mind, and his minnow is the stuff of the soul. We think with figures of speech, he thinks with images: If the skull is a shell, the bird is the thought.

Graves is an experience in the uncommonplace. He speaks to the imagination, and you wonder inevitably about the man. He is needed to connect two worlds, that of his painting and that of daily existence. To be sure, too dogged an account will miss the man altogether, and he cannot be tramped after by a biographer or he will not be there. But it tells as much to see the man as to talk paintings.

He comes from the Pacific Northwest; an exceedingly tall thin figure, with large transfixed, rather alarmed eyes, Graves wears a close-trimmed full beard, and there is something of D. H. Lawrence, grown double height in the Northwest climate. He is shy and self-aware to a degree, aloof, yet (you suspect) ruthless in his self-determination. He seems devoid of the secret embarrassment of being born an artist, and has no desire whatever to be like anyone else. "Making your own life," is a recurrent phrase.

His privacy is defended by many hurdles and warnings. Purposeful ruts are left deep in the road by which you approach his house, and signs say no trespassing, no peddlers, no unauthorized persons, in short: No. The final hurdle is Graves's ritualistic politeness, a self-restraint which is limited by his sense of farce. In short, he is very *birdlike:* receding, private, mobile, and migratory. He is birdlike with his different, yet natural, control over the space we share; but mostly, on reflection, he has the willful steely quality of a bird—its capacity to survive.

You are meeting him in the region north of Seattle from which he comes.

1

His home is deep in hundred-foot trees, the building his own handiwork, an extravaganza in protective space by a man who has always opposed himself to "middle-class gregariousness." Follow him at once into his studio, which is workmanlike, and realize that it is an ordeal for him to throw it open. The place is bare, the walls white. Outside the window there is a dwarfed pine, symbol of the "concentrated treatment of nature in Japan," and immediately beyond is a high white wall. A stove, high tables at which he can work standing, a few odd accidental objects, a Giotto print on the wall, something of Siena, and two ambivalent photographs from Chartres, a demon and a Christ.

There are sheaves of drawings: black chalk, charcoal, pencil on tan paper, kept with the casualness with which they were created. There are fragments from the various periods: the Inner Eye birds, the Journeys, the Pines. A roll of the early oils is of interest: a Red Calf Series—symbolism even before he had recognized his trade. One feels something being taken captive in the drawings and paintings, and Graves—uneasily hovering over his disrupted privacy—seems to be struggling to tame himself.

On the wall there is a sort of credo. Quotations from Chinese painters of the Sung period, which conclude with the words of Ni Tsan:

> *Powerful and full of feeling*
> *Subtle and expressive of thought*
>
> *Light as floating clouds*
> *Vigorous as a startled dragon*
>
> *His ideas are like clouds floating in space,*
> *or a stream hurrying along—perfectly natural*
>
> *Zen means for a man to behold his own*
> *fundamental nature*
>
> *What I call painting is no more than a*
> *careless fantasy of the*
> *brush, not aiming at resemblance*
> *but only at the diversion of the*
> *painter.*

LITTLE-KNOWN BIRD OF THE INNER EYE, 1941.
The Museum of Modern Art, New York

FROM THE FIRST

Morris Graves was born on August 28, 1910. That the place was Fox Valley, Oregon, was a vagary in his father's pursuit of the frontier.

"My father was a product of the pre-Klondike Seattle boom; at twenty-nine to thirty he believed that his fortune was made. He was extravagant. He bought horses at the Seattle-Yukon Exposition. He was excited about Percherons. He had a paint business, the Seattle Paint and Paper Company, and his interest in Percherons took him into the Seattle Transfer Company. He had a Whitmanesque, chest-bared-to-the-storm attitude toward the West and he bought a large tract of grazing and sagebrush land near Baker, Oregon, planning to retire there. Mother had been born and brought up in Seattle, and she was not a frontierwoman. She disagreed with the Fox Valley idea. But she stayed there fifteen months, in the course of which I was born. Then she picked up the children and fled. She refused to go back, my father's plans collapsed, and the family returned to Seattle.

"My father went back into business, but as he grew older, he followed more and more the pattern of his own nature. He became involved in prospecting and mining ventures in remote sections. Reality dissolved in expectation, and there was often a mystery about his absences." (Graves, like his father, is nomadic, and if he has quarreled with the wilderness and reproached it for its lacks, it has fed his spirit, and he has sought it when he needed strength.)

Morris was the sixth child of eight. "From two to seven I was thought to be not long for this world, and there was a background of special treatment. My supposed frail health and my moodiness created a sort of history or attitude in the family, and my particular interests were seen as a carry-over from it. The family finally felt that I was designed by nature never to accomplish anything that they held valuable."

He went to school in Richmond Highlands on the north side of Seattle. An early year was lost to illness, and at seventeen, after two years of high school and one summer spent as an ordinary seaman, he decided to turn to the sea. He applied for a seaman's job without his family's knowledge and then deliberately "created a disturbance" at school. "There was a plan, and the result was partially foreseen. The principal suggested that—what with

SURF BIRDS, 1940
The Detroit Institute of Arts

SURF BIRD, *ca.* 1940
Mr. and Mrs. Charles Laughton,
Hollywood

WOODPECKERS, 1940
The Seattle Art Museum

my disinterest and artistic nature—I had better be away for a while. My parents believed, too, that some very hard knocks were needed. I received notice from the shipping company that they had a place for a cadet seaman. They must have wanted one badly."

The boy made two trips to the East during the winter and the spring months. He saw Tokyo and its environs, Shanghai, Hong Kong, the Philippine and Hawaiian Islands. "Too much has been made of these early trips to the Orient. I made no drawings at the time. I was interested in the Spanish colonial architecture in Manila, and in the gardens of Japan. You could get out into the countryside from Tokyo—it was only half an hour by train. In Japan I at once had the feeling that this was the right way to do everything. It was the acceptance of nature—not the resistance to it. I had no sense that I was to be a painter, but I breathed a different air." On the last homeward passage he landed in San Francisco, a city he was to get to know well; and he hitchhiked home along the coast.

He was unable to settle down, and he now set out for New Orleans with the further idea of going to Mexico. New Orleans had long been in his boyish mind as a sort of cultural mirage contrasting with the world he had known. He saw it as a center of urbanity, established, interested in art. "I had been driven by the uncultivated aspect of the Northwest. The way we think of Alaska was the way I felt about Puget Sound. There was no enrichment in music, the theater, architecture, or gardening. I was in search of a cultivated life, an established history, of any place away from Seattle. (Yet my home environment, the climate, and particularly the weather, pulled me back. Our weather is the most remarkable phenomenon: the thing which brings me back to the Northwest. The way weather occurs here—you get into it like an old coat.)"

He had a friend in Los Angeles from his sailing days. Graves stopped there on his roundabout way. Sketchbooks exist from this time. He made notations in Griffith Park Zoo and he journeyed to the zoo in San Diego. In the sketchbooks there are donkeys looking through the bars of the lined paper, but most of the drawings are of birds. The first gesture of talent can be mysterious; line is everything from the beginning; it is like watching a young cowboy working with a rope: a snarl, a loop, and suddenly it surrounds and captures a thing that is alive, which cannot escape.

Still bent on New Orleans, his next stop was in Beaumont, Texas, where he dropped in to see an aunt—simply to call and have a bath. His aunt and uncle were perhaps "most representative of what was puritanical and recti-linear in the family." They worked upon him and persuaded him that if he did not at least finish high school, his "life would run out the wide end of a bottle." So he stayed with them and finished high school in Beaumont, and by way of compensation he began to paint. "I illustrated the school art annual with symbolic birds and got a diploma for doing it. I did not fulfill the mathematics requirements, but being older and bigger than most of the high school kids, I was sent on through to graduation."

At the time, he received a book on modern art, which his aunt pronounced to be garbage. This prompted Graves "to go to the garbage can and rescue objects of beauty: eggshells, orange peels, etc., to explain to my aunt that there were no degrees in beauty." After graduation he went to New Orleans for the summer months.

New Orleans, myth and fact. That summer of 1932, he lived with the Bult-man family in their great classic revival house. Fritz Bultman, who grew up to be a painter, was then eight or nine, and the young Graves of twenty-one showed him a little about painting. "I was happy and fortunate to be in such a home, but New Orleans did not work out for me. The city brought me up against my upbringing. The Bohemian life, the sensuality, the endless talk, the lounging and postponements turned me away with a sense of contamina-tion. I came back to Edmonds, to the family. The Depression was beginning to be felt."

His father had recently built a summer house in Edmonds, to the north of Seattle, and there the family now moved. "Hard times brought us back from one direction or another. I threw in my lot with the painter, Guy Ander-son, and we improvised our life."

Graves was then working in rough, bold patterns on sacking, the exposed mesh contrasting with the heavy paint. The key was low and the whites carrying; objects were detached decorative entities. Graves, who was trying out symbols, could reach unashamedly for the paraphernalia of the surreal-ists—there is a Daliesque table with a human foot. For the best in this kind, Moor Swan won the prize in the Seattle Art Museum's Northwest Annual in October of 1933. On the prize money from Moor Swan the two painters

8

rented a stable in Seattle and converted it into a studio; come summer they made a camp in the mountains where they painted.

"I had my first help from Dr. Richard Fuller of the Seattle Museum at about this time. I took a painting to Fuller and asked him to buy it. It was of a Dalmatian bitch with very relaxed teats—oil on canvas, painted in much the manner of the gander [Moor Swan] that won the prize in Seattle. But it was not an attractive subject to Fuller, who gave me seventy-five dollars instead of buying it, and said he would give me another seventy-five whenever I needed it." The Dalmatian was painted at the stable studio. Still Life and Summer Still Life tell us more of this early style, and show us a Graves already content with a pattern of separate arresting objects.

Moor Swan, 1933
The Seattle Art Museum

"In the spring [of 1934] Guy Anderson and I got a twenty-five dollar truck—a Model-T laundry truck which served as a camp and a studio—and a life of drift and adventure began. We took six months going to Los Angeles in the truck, led on by the thought that we might possibly have a show there. We lived by occasional hay harvesting or berry-picking. At that time we were deep in the Depression—many buildings were abandoned, with much or little of their furnishings left behind, and we collected antiques."

Los Angeles, in the autumn of 1934: Anderson and Graves still lived in the truck, but eventually they sold it for five or ten dollars and moved in with friends. Then Anderson left, and Graves stayed on in Los Angeles alone. "For a while I rented a basement on Sunset Boulevard, from fashionable furriers overhead. I was allowed to occupy the one basement room, but I was forbidden to cook. This was the Depression: I was cooking onions, and the only client the furriers had seen for weeks was driven out. I was ordered out on the spot, and the two women stood over me until I got out. I combed Beverly Hills for servants' houses and garden houses, offering to do yard work. Owners were holing up in kitchens and dining rooms to save fuel and light, and if they kept their places up a little, it was in hope of a sale. Finally, I got a gardener's house at a vacant place and kept the garden in order, in case some buyer came to look.

"While I lived under the furriers, I sold a still life to a scenario writer. The painting was for an overmantle, and I had to antique it, so I varnished it and put dust and dirt on the wet varnish; and there was still another sale, a painting of tuberoses for a beauty parlor on Sunset." Of more interest, Graves painted a six-panel screen, of Dalmatians now reinforced with harlequin great Danes, against a Giottoesque view of the Hollywood hills. "This same scenario writer knew Katharine Hepburn. Everybody was trying to help everyone in those days and there was some arrangement for me to take the panels around. The stretchers were seven feet by thirty inches—six panels. I set them up in the home of Katharine Hepburn who was out at the time. Soon the scenario writer's wife came around, saying that Katharine Hepburn had seen them and demanded that they be taken out at once. There were eight or more dogs, very hangdog, with bloodshot eyes, running through the landscape." The panels no longer exist, but the Moor Swan and the Still Life's suggest their carrying power.

10

FISH REFLECTED UPON OUTER AND MENTAL SPACE, 1943
Mr. and Mrs. Charles Laughton, Hollywood

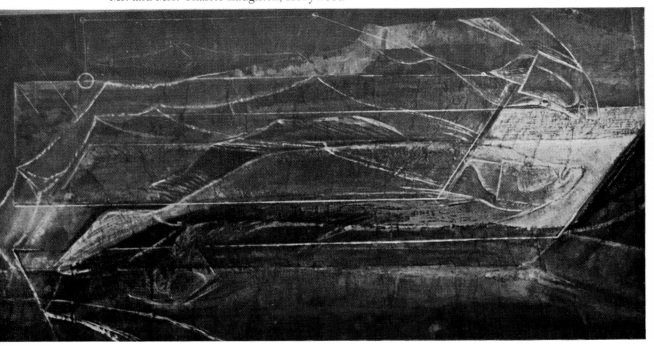

There was a difficult transition in Graves—we must return to it—from a decorative interest in surface to a subsurface, an altogether subjective interest in meaning, from the extensive to the intensive, from large to small. From characteristics Graves moved to character and then to the evocation of a personality all the more mysterious in that it was lodged in nonhuman life.

It was February, 1935. Graves received a telegram telling him of his father's death. He returned to Seattle. It was the end of a venture.

That summer Graves painted a Sunflower Series. In the only example seen, the paint is heavy and full, with something of Van Gogh and Gauguin swept together, and the somber key the only thing of Graves. The young artist is struggling to explore relationships in architectural space, and the painting at least makes clear to us that this is not Graves's true employment. The images which he will soon evoke will establish relationships with each other (and with us) because of their nature and not because of their position. The mature Graves is not concerned with problems of gravity, structure, and place as they affect other forms of art.

But stay with Graves's circumstances in these days, "The Depression had brought three of my brothers home. The house was full. We had built a kind of bunkhouse on my father's place that we called Bachelors' Quarters. I converted this building into a studio." It is still thought of as a beautiful studio by those who knew it, for Graves has the capacity to "control space and to balance order and fantasy." Or perhaps the place looms in retrospect, since it no longer exists. "When it came time for a housewarming I had Guy Anderson and two Chinese painters in from Seattle. I went back to Seattle with them and the studio burned that night. I lost all that I had"—including the Dalmatians and the Danes.

With his home crowded and the studio gone, Graves took a room in an

Dying Pigeon Series, 1939
Mr. and Mrs. Charles Laughton, Hollywood

old house in Seattle for the winter and he began again. The Federal Art Project had been set up by this time, but it was not until the following spring of 1936 that it was a resource to him. It was to tide Graves over for the next few years, and you have the impression of winters bringing him back to the city and to government support. He was in Puyallup Valley (a little way south of Seattle) in the summer of 1936, where he painted a Red Calf Series, a half step forward from the Sunflower paintings of the year before.

Graves is one of the Federal Art Project's rewards for patience with an artist's struggle to develop, and a Message Series, painted for the project in 1937, brings a complete change, in scale, in subtlety, but above all in the relationships between images, which now seem simply afloat in the bloodstream of creation. It is misleading to call this new Graves a surrealist. He senses, rather, the evocative power of forms. If the control of symbols separates man from the animals, Graves wrestles with this mystery, making an animal (poignantly) a symbol of something which can evolve out of itself, but which it can never understand.

Works done under the Federal Art Project were assembled in Washington, D.C., and were there seen in 1939 by Dorothy C. Miller and Alfred H. Barr, Jr., of the Museum of Modern Art. Recognizing the significance of what they saw, they chose four of Graves's paintings, the Message Series, for inclusion in a group show drawn from the project. Graves had hardly been ready for discovery when he was discovered.

At this time (in the spring of 1939 when Graves was in New York) he made the seven drawings of a dying pigeon in the Mr. and Mrs. Charles Laughton Collection. Here he is suddenly as good as he comes, and yet this handwriting is only a firming up of the first sketchbook drawings in Griffith Park. The theme of death seems to clean up the line, just as death itself can pare the image to the bone.

BIRD IN THE MIST, 1937
Mr. and Mrs. Roy R. Neuberger, New York

BLIND BIRD, NO. 1, 1940
The Museum of Modern Art, New York

THE CHOICE OF INFLUENCES

The Northwest faces the East; the breadth of the Pacific is not a solid dimension. The Oriental is a living part of the Coastal scene, so harmonious within himself, so strikingly incongruous in the landscape, so imbued with a different feeling toward time and change, which breeds such different desires; creating his own ambience wherever two or three are gathered together, a world of half tones, an atmosphere inviting and forbidding. Lumber camps have their Chinese cooks; San Francisco has its Chinatown; Seattle, too, has its visible contacts with the East. Even on the crass physical level an Oriental enters the outgoing Western scene as art enters it, disturbing, not to be imagined were he not a fact.

The response to the East is not confined to the artist. Buddhism has its devotees; swamis have their audiences; the presence of the East compensates for the frontier's lack. Doubtless the responses are on various levels, from the naïve to the aware. It was the good fortune of the artists of the region that they had before their eyes Oriental art of front-rank quality to lift them above the fumes of cult. They could see the growing collections of the Seattle Art Museum. To take the evidence of one painter, as Guy Anderson remembers his student days, the museum's Oriental collections were all that was worth the seeing.

Anderson was deeply imbued with Eastern art, and the young Graves found him "living in a philosophic world, religion, etc., out of my reach." Anderson recalls a Graves having more feeling than himself, a-thirst for information. Said Graves: "Anderson had had formal training in painting and his skill and knowledge of materials were very generously given."

Then there was the short-lived Sherrill Van Cott, a young sculptor and painter who was a close friend from 1939 to 1943. Van Cott's gifted minor key paintings offered some quality of twilight alertness, of perceptive restraint in grays, browns, and off-whites. Graves "responded" to Van Cott's work and the two men were often together. We must come back to Van Cott in his brief time.

The major formative influence upon Graves—at least among painters—was Mark Tobey. A Northwest painter nearly a generation older than Graves, Tobey is of a caliber to cast an influence over younger men. Graves seems

CONCENTRATED PINE TOP, 1944
Mr. Dan R. Johnson, New York

DOVE OF THE
INNER EYE, 1941
Private Collection,
New York

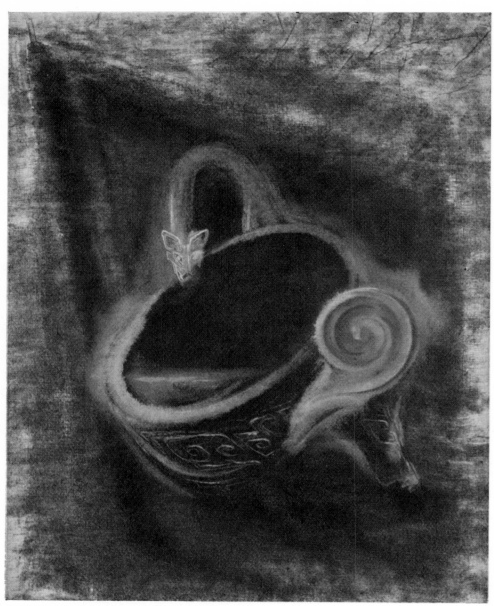

INDIVIDUAL STATE OF THE WORLD, 1947
The Museum of Modern Art, New York

to have met Tobey soon after his father's death, the burning of the studio, and the new start. Tobey had recently returned from Japan "where he had steeped himself in Japanese aesthetics." To wed something of the East to abstract art was in effect to circumnavigate the globe. The painters became friends, interested in each other's work. "Tobey had sensitivity, a Japanese-conditioned approach to nature, intuitive power"—all things which Graves admires. For both men, Eastern art, Eastern thought, offered something between a discipline and a key to their particular abilities. The time was soon to come when Graves would bend to his own mystical purposes a distinctive mode of expression, *white writing*, which Tobey was developing, but from the first they had this common bond in the East.

Zen Buddhism has been one of Graves's resources, providing his mysticism with justification, order, and a name. "Zen stresses the meditative, stilling the surface of the mind and letting the inner surface bloom." Graves feels that activity obliterates the meditative vision which comes from living alone in nature. He is scornful of the pursuit of knowledge for its own sake, and believes that the duty of man is "lifting his own consciousness," so that "knowledge of his origin and destination is in some way reached."

He describes the earliest turn in this direction frankly enough: "My family was religious, we were members of a church barren of beauty, and I could not sustain an interest in their affiliation. Taoism, Buddhism, East Indian religious systems, all seemed to me immeasurably superior—lifting me beyond my family's spiritual rewards. Now that that has simmered for years I am growing in my awareness of Christianity as a religious system, a superb insight into human nature."

"Zen Buddhism" seems to be a phrase steeped in Graves's own purposes. It offers him not only the self-realization he seeks, but it exalts intuition, which is a resource, at the expense of introspection, which can become an obstacle. "I would not want to examine into motives," says Graves at this point—with a warning glance—"should not want to turn the psychological attitude of mind on myself. I think it is possible for one section of your mind, the rational, to intrude upon yourself and hamper deeper insight. We can acquire a certain knowledge of our behavior, but I am in disagreement with that. I believe in living by the intuitional aspect of your nature."

This brings us to the other major influence: the person who has meant and

19

means most to him is a woman—"who has had the largest influence in my life." The friendship adapted itself to Graves's ruthless drive toward independence, and so survived. Graves has given himself (so far as it is possible, granted a major dedication) and in return has received much of his awareness and experience of music: Bach, Verdi, Vivaldi. His friend has offered, too, much of experience as opposed to mood in the absorption of Zen philosophy. They read together: the Japanese Noh plays, and Chinese and Japanese poetry; chanoyu or the Zen so-called Tea Ceremony; and Fenollosa's *Epochs of Chinese and Japanese Art*. "We were attracted by Zen wit, the insight through paradoxes, the jest and humor in the riddle of creation." Graves feels that she brought home to him the sense of the oneness of the universe. "She was absorbed in Buddhism, and in the Christian mystics and saints."

CEREMONIAL BRONZE TAKING THE FORM OF A BIRD, 1947
The Seattle Art Museum

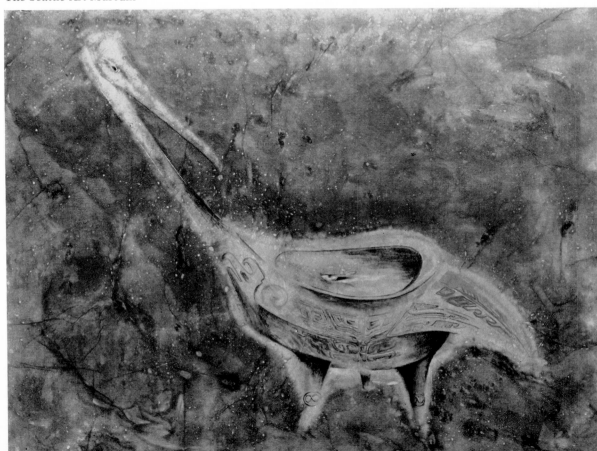

THE DEVICES OF SOLITUDE

Led on by his instinct for detachment, chivied by the difficulties of the times, Graves now retreated to the town of La Conner on Puget Sound, some forty or fifty miles north of Seattle. His isolation for the next few years should not be overstressed. He had friends who came to see him; he was in Seattle every two months or so. Yet his solitude, his remoteness, were definitely a means. For Graves, who fed out of himself, solitude was nourishing. He achieved some control of his circumstances and of himself—inner and outer bound together by technical resources which were found at the right time, too. His painting was developing not so much by recognizable growth as by unpredictable metamorphosis; at one stage it was earthbound, at another, it was not. It is not too strange if in the interim he was wrapped up in himself.

When Graves came to La Conner the population had slumped from five hundred to one hundred, and vacant and paintless houses could be had cheap enough. Being by now used to abandoned nests, he took a two-story house which had been half burned out. "How I lived I can't recall. When the Federal Art Project folded I hadn't saved anything. I had an occasional sale—meant as an act of charity. But by 1938 I had found a way of life. You anticipate the things that are going to be meaningful. You resort to what you can produce with the greatest satisfaction." BIRD IN THE MIST of the Roy and Marie Neuberger Collection sets the mood for these years.

He commented on the Munich Conference with the Museum of Modern Art's four NIGHTFALL PIECES: BRITISH, FRENCH, ROMAN, and GERMAN. They are satires. "Thinking back, you felt the mood of the world for war. You were not too close to society so as to be identified with it. You were concerned with the state of the world; you found that living on the sidelines more than you had previously was a very 'opening'—a productive sort of experience. It helped accomplish an attitude or state of mind. The Depression and the isolation—we were all experiencing a kind of despair—and then this new environment up here changed a gear. You didn't have to end up with zero."

There was nothing local in Graves's awareness, and with the mere turn of a season Graves was able to migrate as far as he wished, to take wing, seemingly without effort or resource. He was in La Conner for the summer; autumn came, and he decided on Puerto Rico. Off he went.

To reach Puerto Rico he passed through New York. It was not his first visit to the city. There had been a feckless jalopy-jaunt from San Francisco to New York some time before 1937, but it had added up to nothing but mileage. On his second sight of New York, Graves visited a number of galleries and the Museum of Modern Art.

In Puerto Rico he painted the Purification Series, and the very title—moral, ritualistic, suggesting that peace must be found within, that there are ways of living with the world without surrendering to it—has the sound of the mature Graves.

Here in a series of temperas or gouaches a kind of communion-taking goes on before our eyes. The image of a chalice—private symbol of Graves's for spiritual birth—becomes ingested in some magma of igneous rock, and appears progressively to bring the amorphous mass into sentient life.

He was living in San Juan, opposite the cathedral. "I was there at the time of the death of the Pope. There is no doubt but that the daily Catholic ritual had its influence upon me." It was probably at this time he added to the Nightfall Series with PAPAL NIGHTFALL PIECE.

You see Graves still caught between the intensive and extensive: he was certainly still painting large, and he speaks of selling a "decorative" painting. When he came to leave—after six months—he was embarrassed by the scale of his efforts. It was a question whether to pack or abandon. Graves had come to know some of the local strugglers in paint, and in his quandary he gave away his largest works in response to the wild enthusiasm of a fellow artist. "The man fell on his knees and wept, and confessed that he had never dreamed of possessing such large canvases to paint on." This interlude over, Graves returned to Seattle.

PURIFICATION SERIES, 1938–1939
Mrs. Marian Willard Johnson, New York

GUARDIAN, 1952
The University of Illinois, Champaign-Urbana

CHALICE AND LYRE, 1942
Mr. John S. Newberry, Jr., Grosse Pointe, Michigan

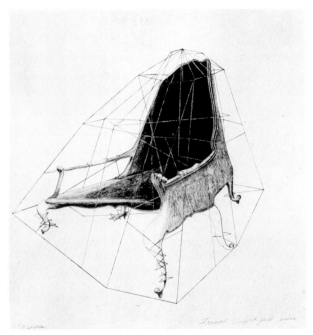

FRENCH NIGHTFALL PIECE, 1938
The Museum of Modern Art, New York

Shore Birds, No. 1,
ca. 1940
Private Collection,
New York

Shore Birds, No. 2,
ca. 1940
Mr. Lee Foley,
Evanston, Illinois

It was April. He was painting falling chalices (he writes at this time) and was working with encaustic wax over tempera. We have come to the year of MOON CHALICE of the Mr. and Mrs. Charles Laughton Collection, of the Museum of Modern Art's SNAKE AND MOON and BIRD SINGING IN THE MOONLIGHT. The Inner Eye Series was only two years away. The region where these paintings occurred is important. They should be discovered in their matrix. Graves himself served as guide.

The San Juan Islands are crumbs of mountains strewn through the fogs of Puget Sound. Fidalgo, where Graves was to build and live, is cut off from the mainland and La Conner by no more than a river or moat. Graves sees the islands as totally different in nature, in rock formation, from the neighboring land which has washed down from the Cascades. He makes much of this. "The stone gives the forests a quality of permanence and order." The outer islands are thought to screen away the persistent rain of the Northwest and the region lays special claim to the sun.

Fidalgo does not appear as an island until you reach the bridge. On the mainland side La Conner makes out with lumbering and waits for a main highway which is approaching with its sordid opportunities. The town, incidentally, has no French ancestry; it was named for its founder, an Irishman, L. A. Conner. Graves points to the house which he once owned, and we go on to the island where he came to terms with the wilderness. He took the writer to the scene in an effort to make all plain; and if he did so with reluctance, it was distressing to him to return. Rolling north by truck, we were aware of the absurdity of looking for the evidence of a half-forgotten struggle with creation as though it were an external thing, complete with footprints of full-moon walks in the forests. Yet both felt that the trail led somewhere, that something had happened hereabouts. Graves spoke soberly of going to The Rock—his name for both a place and the camp which he had built. The road on which he had labored went lurching over ledges and was now so overgrown that the truck harvested the small trees in its path.

At the summit of the island the high woods opened and a bronze and sunlit carpet of pine needles warmed the gray stone outcroppings. Here the ground fell away in every direction—there is something Oriental in a landscape too precipitous for climbing yet rounded as moss. A linear accretion of sheds followed the edge of a cliff, recessed to make room for the great trees which grew up from beyond the brink. For the better part of the time that Graves was here there had been only one room, built from salvaged lumber "for the effect of lichen and weather. The places I inhabited had to have particular qualifications of location and privacy and . . . weathered surfaces. I abhor the environment which suits the average nomad—the migrant agricultural workers and vagrants and bohemian philosophical drifters."

Returning, Graves looked on the scene with the wonder a man feels at the effort he once made to meet needs all but forgotten: Why did I do this, how is all changed, how have I changed? He seemed to be taking his bearings. The larger rocks which appeared to be strewn here by nature were in reality sweated into a studied and deliberate arrangement, as he pointed out. "There is an experience still very far beyond the grasp of the Western mind in the poetic statements of repose in nature which you see in Japanese stone gardens. They are the only masterpieces of their kind." Finding a soft spot of earth which satisfied him, he suddenly dug with purpose and produced a key, and he opened up the camp.

The Rock was warping and moldering under its tar paper, and there were a few blackened remnants of paintings. The windows looked straight down a stone cliff the length of a valley, across an intimate and private lake, southwesterly into the sun, and offered a glimpse of Puget Sound. In the other direction, you walked to a view of the snowy Cascades. On the north side, too, there was a little lake with an island. Graves once bought the island for five dollars.

The original shack was built in 1940 with the help of Sherrill Van Cott, already mentioned for his sensitive paintings. Van Cott, a younger man, lived with his family some thirty miles away, but he was often at The Rock. "He saw my paintings in Seattle and sent me a note. We took to each other. He saw things the way I saw things." Van Cott had a heart condition, and he had died by 1943. His paintings have since been exhibited—Graves saw to it—and there is still a stack of them in Graves's studio. He existed in his own right, a genuine talent.

One of Graves's resources in this period was white writing, and with the marvelous BIRD SINGING IN THE MOONLIGHT in mind, we must return to Mark Tobey. Graves's painting was in existence by 1939, and by this time white writing had emerged in the work of both artists—Graves apparently

EAGLE IN THE ROCK, 1941
Mr. Robert M. Shields, Seattle

BIRD IN THE MOONLIGHT, 1940
Nancy Wilson Ross
(Mrs. Stanley Young),
Old Westbury, Long Island

SHORE BIRDS SUBMERGED
IN MOONLIGHT, *ca.* 1940
Dr. William R. Valentiner,
Los Angeles

adapting to his purposes a technical device which was already in existence in Tobey's work.

Beginnings are obscure, but here is one account. Graves was shown in Tobey's studio a circular white design on brown paper, an experiment which Tobey called his "Doodle Doily." The thing caught Graves's imagination, and he "related" it to an experience of his own. At The Rock, Graves had a rain barrel "for a water catchment" which reflected a circular pattern of trembling sunlight on the ceiling when the door stood open. Graves had felt the hypnotism of this image, all the more compelling in that it was evanescent, immaterial, made of light alone. He saw now that it might be captured in the mesh of the Doodle Doily.

With so much impetus, Graves embarked on a series which was to develop into the Moonlight and Inner Eye paintings. Graves and Tobey are basically very different artists and of course white writing was entirely different in the hands of each. For Graves white writing provided an aura or ambience in which his symbols could nest; for Tobey it had been a much more structural thing, for a while the very fabric of his work.

Bird Singing in the Moonlight is a theme several times repeated, one example belonging to Nancy Wilson Ross (Mrs. Stanley Young), another to Dorothy C. Miller, a third to the Museum of Modern Art. Here is the white writing, but in Graves the writing is audible, the image of a song, as certain lyrics in the language leave the page and enter the ear by way of the eye. It is an image of unaccountable happiness. Night, fragility, and solitude promise danger and produce joy.

Graves led a nocturnal existence at The Rock, tramping under a full moon until midnight, as we are told, then returning to paint until morning. You have the impression that each new discovery in paint is a night scene, and then the scene clears up as though the eye had become accustomed to this twilight and dawn world. In the Shore Birds subject, for instance—again three versions, one belonging to Lee Foley, another to Alfred H. Barr, Jr., a third to Miss Elodie Courter (Mrs. Robert Osborn)—there is a low but clear light, as though we had begun with night and progressed to the peculiar illumination of the dream. There is the same dream distortion, too, which curiously intensifies recognition instead of destroying it.

Graves, pressed on his relation to nature, remarked that the bird is a symbol of solitude, the shore, of the environment of childhood—"the way down to the shore is near here." But this is missing the heart of the matter. "I am not so much a naturalist as some people suppose," he added.

To weigh subtleties, BLIND BIRD is a masterpiece on a level with BIRD SINGING IN THE MOONLIGHT. Impotence, in some manifestation, has been the price of innocence, in art and life, from the beginning of time, but in art it is often turgidly managed; and it has never been more simply handled than here. The denial of function is a spiritual function. The blind see for us; the mute sing, too. But in BLIND BIRD the white writing of song has sunk down about the creature's feet, as though it were bird lime. "The blind darkness written on our mind and heart can be so dark that the very ground is luminous in comparison." This subject, too, exists in two versions, equally fine: one in the Museum of Modern Art, the other in the collection of Mr. and Mrs. Robert T. Markson.

Graves of course works in series, and to mention one or two examples is to select, perhaps without justification. One of the best of the moonlight–white-writing paintings is in Dr. Valentiner's collection of Graves.

All this is preparation for the LITTLE-KNOWN BIRD OF THE INNER EYE. This red painting is an image on the retina, the place where the seen bird actually exists. Its eyes have the mysterious range-finding aspect of human eyes; it sees two-pronged. It has four legs—as though it had suddenly moved and stopped. This bird has a strict invented form (it is Graves's most formal painting to this date), and this form, like the form of a real bird, sustains its power.

Graves has this to offer: "The images seen within the space of the inner eye are as clear as 'seeing stars' before your eyes if you get up suddenly. It is certain that they are subjective, yet there is the absolute feeling that they are outside around your head. This is the nearest analogy to the spatializing of the inner eye."

"Do you know Coomaraswamy's writing about the three Spaces? Phenomenal Space, Mental Space, and the Space of Consciousness? . . . Creative artists and critics and laymen must some day learn to recognize from which one of these spaces the painting or sculpture or thought images have been drawn. Not all paintings have their origin in the experiences of Phenomenal Space."

In September of 1940 Graves received further help from Dr. Fuller; but Graves, who desired nothing so much as freedom, was not easy to help. Dr.

32

Fuller offered him a job in the museum, and Graves, indebted to Dr. Fuller as he was, felt embarrassed to refuse. But he did not want to give up his time to a job and become a Sunday painter. A man is what he does. "I accepted, but I made a condition with myself that I would not shave until Fuller invited me to leave. Fuller suggested several times that I shave"—tentatively, you imagine, since Graves was able to turn the subject. "I worked there four months and saved almost the whole of my salary. That was fine."

Graves now discovered that a beard was "a wonderful antisocial barrier, so I kept it on. It was good for more than freeing me from a routine job." Doubtless out of gratitude—since his beard won him his independence—Graves gilded it for Christmas.

BLIND BIRD, No. 2, 1940
Mr. and Mrs. Robert T. Markson, Boston

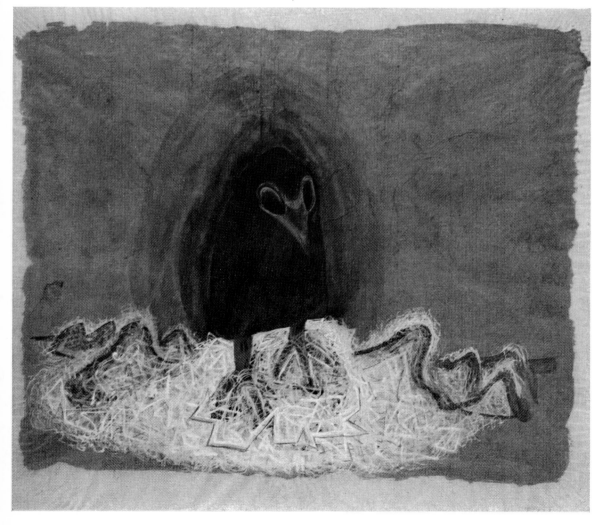

SERIES AND THEMES

Until La Conner and the BIRD SINGING IN THE MOONLIGHT, Graves's work had been fragmentary. From now on his series have a continuity of their own; they lose the air of experiment and appear as consecutive and related preoccupations. It is time for Graves to achieve this freedom from circumstance, for the outer world is now to press more closely upon him. The artist struggles against indifference, yet anonymity is a protection. When he becomes known he becomes vulnerable. In what manner do we catch the eye of Polyphemus and become recognized as an individual and not one of his sheep? The first pressures of success bore down upon Graves in wartime, simultaneously with his experience of the uniform and communal violence. Freedom, he was to discover, was an internal thing, not a circumstance but a state of mind. Solitude was no longer identical with the wilderness—if we stay with Graves's thinking, we are now confronted with an inner and outer space.

He had been *seen*. Dr. Richard Fuller had long taken an interest in Graves and the Seattle Art Museum had given him a one-man show when he was twenty-five—surely an early and encouraging gesture. The Federal Art Project had sustained him; because of it Graves had been included in a group show at the Museum of Modern Art. In that same year of 1939 Marian Willard, his present dealer, was in Seattle visiting Nancy Wilson Ross, who took her to see Graves's work at La Conner. "She took marvelously to my things," said Graves. "She was one of the first to be so concerned."

"Then Dorothy Miller came to Seattle." She of course already knew Graves's paintings, and she wished to see more. "Mark Tobey telephoned my mother's home where I happened to be at the time and I carried around what was available. I had some finished Birds of the Inner Eye, but they were up at The Rock. This was in 1941."

The result of the visit was Graves's inclusion in the Museum's *Americans 1942* exhibition. "Alfred Barr sent me a check for a thousand dollars. I thought, I can build the shelter I need. I spent it building the rest of The Rock." The exhibition (from January 21 through March 8) brought Graves up to date with thirty-four examples of his work. The Messages were represented, the Purification Series, the Chalices, and the Moons; then there were

34

the recent Bird in the Moonlight paintings, and five of the still more recent Inner Eye Series. The early works in heavy paint were passed over. What was shown was in tempera on paper. Entirely personal and self-sufficient, these subtle paintings stood comparison with the art of the East which they recalled, and they announced Graves as one of the foremost painters in America.

Soon after this exhibition, Graves was inducted into the Army, only to be discharged in April, 1943, when he returned to The Rock.

For most men military life is a heightening experience; in retrospect at least they recognize a world of purpose larger than themselves. But for Graves's essentially religious nature there was no such reward. Even in religion whatever was organized was beyond his use. It was a time of self-preservation rather than expansion, and when it was past he was deeply withered. But he now had an inner solitude of his own to match that of his habitat. For a number of months he lived on the Olympic Peninsula, where he painted without cessation. The works of this period are dark and depressed. IN THE NIGHT of the Mr. and Mrs. Charles Laughton Collection, with its large black bird, is typical. So, too, is the disturbing and impressive MOON MAD CROW IN THE SURF of the Milton Lowenthal Collection. Toward the end of the phase, in the important MESSAGE belonging to Marian Willard Johnson, there is a progression out of darkness toward light and color. A bird haunted and shrouded in blackness moves into half light rearmed with spurs and horned crest, and faces a margin of prismatic dawn.

His next series, the Joyous Young Pines, is his most exuberant. In theme,

MESSAGE, 1943
Mrs. Marian Willard Johnson, New York

YOUNG PINE FOREST IN BLOOM, *ca.* 1950
The Phillips Gallery, Washington, D.C.

MOON MAD CROW IN THE SURF, 1943
Mr. and Mrs. Milton Lowenthal, New York

Eagle, *ca.* 1942
The Phillips Gallery, Washington, D.C.

WOUNDED GULL, 1943
The Phillips Gallery, Washington, D.C.

color, and scale, it is the shout of a young man finding himself alive, and the yellow and green paintings grow before the eyes with the pace of a sunrise. There are especially fine examples in the Stanley J. Wolf and Wright Ludington collections, and in that of the Baltimore Museum of Art.

The Journeys follow (there is an excellent example in the Whitney Museum of American Art), and we are again back in a cobweb of light lines in dark, uneasy paintings that tell us as much as can be told of the thousand impul-

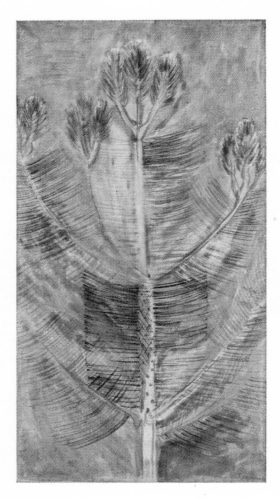

JOYOUS YOUNG PINE, 1943
Mr. and Mrs. Stanley J. Wolf,
Great Neck, New York

sions to migrate. Whether the image is bird or chalice, we are caught in a flowing web which sweeps us away.

Then there are the individual birds of this productive year, each somehow a dramatization of a human trait. To quote Duncan Phillips: "He is familiar with that sardonic owl, that mighty eagle, that moon-crazed crow. His heart has gone out to the young plover fluttering in the shallow surf, and to the old gull, who with twisted plumage and shattered wings sinks at last into his world of boundless sea and sky gone black." One of the finest of this year is Dr. William Valentiner's IN THE AIR, with its two birds touching beak to beak. Duncan Phillips, an early and avid collector, was giving Graves a show at the Phillips Gallery in November, a year after the presentation at the Museum of Modern Art.

Then the Waves—a series of major works, large and full of tumult: the

IN THE AIR, 1943
Dr. William R. Valentiner, Los Angeles

SEA, FISH AND CONSTELLATION of the Seattle Art Museum and the Albright Art Gallery's similar BLACK WAVES; the FISH REFLECTED UPON OUTER AND MENTAL SPACE of the Mr. and Mrs. Charles Laughton Collection, and the PINK FISH AND CONSTELLATION belonging to Paul Peralta-Ramos. The sea is the Pacific—Eastern in style, Western in mass. The tying of the stars with the white lines of a star map is a literary conceit which nevertheless works powerfully—a star map, too, diagrams man's imagination. At sea, man looks to the stars to recognize them, hangs by the constellations and so holds himself above water. SEA AND THE MORNING REDNESS belonging to the Art Institute of Chicago has the same rhythm of the open ocean.

The year 1944 also produced the Leaf Series: sear brown horizontal images of cast-aside lives, which Graves meant as a commentary on interminable war. And from leaf to tree, he returned to the pine theme, but now it is old age: CONCENTRATED OLD PINE TOP of the Mr. and Mrs. John H. Hauberg, Jr. Collection sets the pattern. Graves is now painting large on vertical scrolls intended to hang unframed. A mystical detachment comes into his work as he sets one single object afloat on the surface. He is in his most Eastern phase.

Woundedness now becomes a dramatization of helplessness which stems from the BLIND BIRD. WOUNDED SCOTER, WOUNDED GULL, WOUNDED IBIS: the language of solitude. The exceptional BIRD MADDENED BY THE LONG WINTER of the Stanley J. Wolf Collection sums up this mood. All this time Graves had been living at The Rock.

SEA, FISH AND CONSTELLATION, 1944
The Seattle Art Museum

SEA AND THE MORNING REDNESS, 1944
The Art Institute of Chicago. Gift of Mr. and Mrs. Howard Kornblith
as a memorial to their daughter Suzanne.

Then Graves came down to San Francisco, and met Mischa Dolnicoff who "had the strongest impact on me next to Tobey." We hear of a magnetic temperament able to project such states of mind, identified with Zen and Vedanta, as Graves values most. "He had marvelous insight, a feeling of complete devotion—a way of expanding consciousness. It must be experienced and cannot be talked about. Zen Buddhism comes nearest to apprehending the relationship of man to the universe." You reflect, listening, how remote the sense of the universal is in our day, in a world bludgeoning itself toward unification.

Graves was awarded a Guggenheim Fellowship in the autumn of 1946. His intention was to work and study in Occupied Japan. Before leaving he went to Boston (this was in January, 1947) to see Dr. Ananda K. Coomaraswamy, who had a subtle influence upon him and may have turned his thoughts toward the possibility of continuing an Oriental tradition. Coomaraswamy, it is known, was concerned with the "right use of symbols"—their employment in their traditional meaning and context. At this time too Graves saw an exhibition of Oriental art at the Metropolitan Museum in New York, which must have reinforced his view of an ancient masterpiece as a link in the chain of creation. With such preparation he set sail for Honolulu in February, his mind open to the East.

He did not, however, reach Japan at this time. Instead he stayed in the Islands until July. The Oriental objects in the Honolulu Academy of Art became the Orient that he was seeking, and it was in Honolulu that he created the Chinese Ritual Bronze paintings. They have been wrongly seen as an inward turn: art leaning on art. The fact is that Graves in his persistence found a way to make his Eastern voyage—in the Honolulu Academy of Art.

In accepting the limitation set by the pattern of another work of art Graves is carrying out a ritual already established: if these are religious experiences Graves is here more priest than prophet. Yet—through this very limitation—the works serve to give a precise measure of Graves's originality, of his ability to produce by metamorphosis a later unsuspected stage when the object breaks its cocoon.

In Charles Laughton's DISINTEGRATED AND REANIMATED, "urgency reën-livens, reanimates the head and it turns in contemplation of its disintegrating body (the body of the human race) and meditates upon its vital origin, its once spiritually illuminated past." CEREMONIAL BRONZE TAKING THE FORM OF A BIRD again shows us a live bronze in contemplation, looking back on itself, a vessel which contains a minnow. There will be other minnows, notably in the Metropolitan Museum of Art's SPIRIT BIRD TRANSPORTING MINNOW FROM STREAM TO STREAM. The minnow, for Graves, is that which is creative within us. "When crisis occurs the minnow voluntarily comes into view—to renew faith and give direction. It is then that we can catch him too, or at least . . . memorize his characteristics . . . learn that he is within ourselves." He comes to sight as the bronze vessel lurches, in the Museum of Modern Art's INDIVIDUAL STATE OF THE WORLD.

The collections belonging to Mr. and Mrs. Charles Laughton, Duncan Phillips, Dr. William Valentiner, and the Museum of Modern Art constitute quite distinct responses to Graves's work. The Museum enjoyed the rewards of discovery, and its paintings "relate," as Graves would say, to the awareness of Dorothy Miller and Alfred Barr. No exhibition of Graves can do him justice without the generosity of the Museum of Modern Art.

44

RITUAL VESSEL-MIRROR, 1947
Dr. Kenneth B. Edgers, Seattle

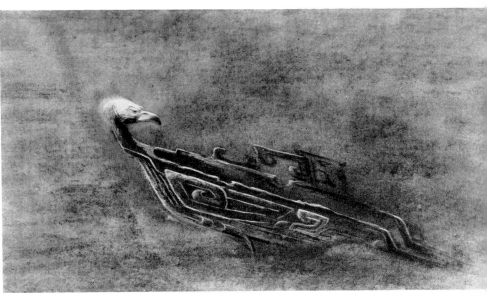

DISINTEGRATED AND REANIMATED, 1947
Mr. and Mrs. Charles Laughton, Hollywood

Masked Bird Fishing in the Golden Stream, 1953
Mr. Garland Ellis, Fort Worth

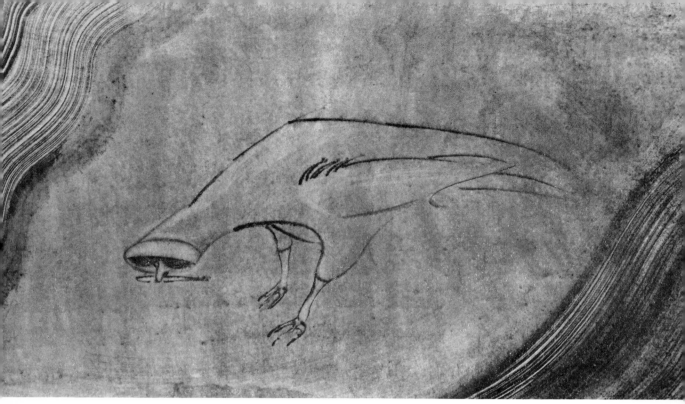

EACH TIME YOU CARRY ME THIS WAY, 1953
Mr. and Mrs. James S. Schramm, Burlington, Iowa

Duncan Phillips was also quick to appreciate Graves's work, and the Phillips Gallery possesses outstanding examples from the 1940's to the present date. He showed Graves early, wrote about him, warmly endorsed his application for the Guggenheim Fellowship. Duncan Phillips is a perceptive translator of things which go difficultly into words. He has been especially aware of meanings as well as of forms, with an eye for the symbol.

Dr. Valentiner is now an old friend of Graves. He has been to The Rock, seeking quality with the instinctive purpose of the bird transporting the minnow, and his group of Graves's works is excellent.

Charles Laughton's response to Graves is a singlehearted thing: he not only has the best and the most of Graves, but these paintings are what he primarily collects. Other painters make out as best they can in a house given over to Graves. Laughton senses a lack in the times which Graves, alone among American painters, is able to fill for him.

47

FORM AND PLACE

A slack period followed the Chinese Bronzes, and Graves was less productive for several years. This coincided with a restlessness which led to a new remove. Graves left The Rock and began to build in Edmonds on property which he had familiarly roamed years before. He wanted "a diagram in space which would seclude," and his impulse has wrung sacrifices from him as he is well aware. As a result, we have the architectural side of a painter actually becoming architecture—of a special sort to be sure, at once personal, romantic, and arbitrary. (Doubtless the architecture of Graves tends to clarify and purify his painting and leave it free for his symbols, just as the painting of a Corbusier tends to draw the symbolism out of his architecture.) Graves has an urge toward elegance, and he achieves his intention regardless, on the principle that one kind of plumage can be grown as cheaply as another.

He began with a gatehouse, a protective entrance or passageway, where he lived while the main house was under construction. Within the entrance it was all a wilderness of hundred-foot trees, pine and maple, second growth clustering out of massive stumps. But do not imagine that the house followed immediately after the completion of the gate. Instead, Graves broke away again, as though in fear that he might entrap himself. When he was settling at The Rock he went off to Puerto Rico; while he was building in Edmonds he went to Europe.

Yet the trip to Europe was not on impulse. There was an intervention in Graves's life. He received a telegram from Edward James, British "collector of Tchelitchew, Dali, and Magritte," inviting him to come to England and do "a dozen lunettes for ten thousand dollars." The painter Carlyle Brown, a mutual friend then staying with Edward James, seems to have suggested this commission. After some reconnoitering, Graves met Edward James in San Francisco and again in New York, and artist and new-found patron sailed on the same ship. The acquaintance, so artificially established, wore out on the voyage, and Graves debarked alone at Cherbourg and went to Paris. He waited, and eventually crossed over to England for a brief period as James's guest. He then came back to France and took a house in Chartres for the winter. There was a trip to Italy in the spring, before he returned home.

48

PINK BIRD, 1951
Mr. and Mrs. Joseph Shapiro, Oak Park, Illinois

In Chartres the cathedral became Graves's theme. But the whole vast epic in glass and exfoliating stone did not translate like the Chinese Bronzes. To quote Kenneth Rexroth's recent perceptive study, "No one has seen what Graves did at Chartres. In conversation he has told me how he spent the better part of a cold foggy winter there, painting every day, details of the cathedral, fragments of statues, bits of lichened masonry, and several pictures of the interior of the cathedral in early morning—the great vault half filled with thick fog, dawn beginning to sparkle in the windows. When he came back to America and reviewed the year's work he destroyed it all."

To be noted here is the self-discipline in such an act. Graves is always restrained, well aware of the risk in facility, the threat in repetition. Paintings in a series add up to a single exploration; and when the vein is exhausted there is an end to the matter. The Chartres paintings did not seem right when they were examined at home.

Back in Edmonds we reënter the gate. The high trees are brilliant green or dank under the Northwest rain clouds; we follow a circle and discover the house, now just completed: a formal doorway, flanked by French windows, is centered in a cement block wall some hundred feet long. Graves opens: the floor of the central hall is still being laid. We go through to a loggia the length of the building, its roof supported by double columns of timber rough-sawn in octagon. The roof is high, but the proportions are so ample that it seems low. At one end of the great porch is the studio; at the other the dining room, kitchen, living quarters. The dining room windows face an extensive lawn, green as only the Northwest allows, a green lake with its own island of high trees and its own shores of forest. The lawn is bordered by a long garden, blue with delphinium. Everything is still in the making, and down at the forest end, large stumps are being pulled and hauled.

The drawing-room (no other word does) has a fourteen-foot ceiling which composes with dimensions roughly twenty by forty. The paneled walls are the Graves snuff color, faintly washed with white. The doors appear to be ten feet high. The chimney in the long wall has a fireplace in black and white Mexican marble, highly polished (the black diamonds on white are a fantasy of Graves's), and the highly polished hearth doubles the fire. Directly above the hearth on the white ceiling is an oval black spot, perhaps a foot across,

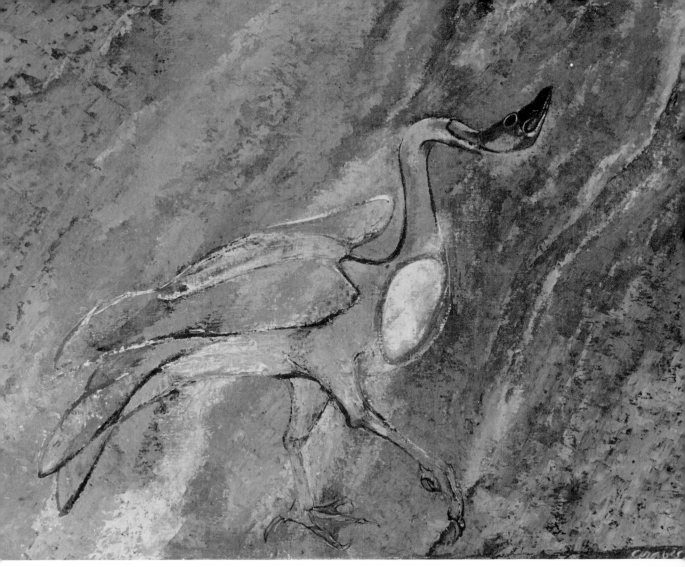

ECSTATIC GANDER, 1952
The Willard Gallery, New York

but its dimensions are incalculable. Once seen, it takes control of the paintingless room. The extraordinary thing about this house is that it has happened. The necessary loans, the actual effort, figure as so much brushwork: it is a Graves.

Graves feels called on for understatement. "A man must live somewhere . . . a place to wash . . . to meet one's friends. . . . Building is not a bad 'activity' art, but it is not the right art. Painting as an activity is the satisfaction. I don't have the same satisfaction in building. But *there is the need to be surrounded by your own shapes, for the control of your own space.*" These phrases recur. Building then is a discipline, and it betokens a clarified grasp of form. It is well to stress this success with the architect's space, since it is not the space which Graves uses in his paintings.

In 1949 Graves produced a Bouquet Series: small paintings, sensitive and subdued, with exquisite lyrics among them. Yet you have the impression of a musician trying his instrument before embarking on a major work.

There was another unproductive excursion during this period. The painter was in Mexico for half a year in 1950.

LOON CALLING ON AN AUTUMN LAKE, 1953
The Willard Gallery, New York

DAISIES, 1949
Mr. and Mrs. Piek Van Waveren, Greenwich, Connecticut

The *new* paintings of the building period are larger oils. The early rough and decorative patterns now fuse with those inward and sensitive images which seem somehow (however absurd in logic) mind-sized instead of life-sized. The best of these are the best Graves. None is better than YOUNG GANDER READY FOR FLIGHT, which exists in two versions, one belonging to the Phillips Gallery, the other in the Mrs. Donald E. Frederick Collection. both of 1952. Mrs. Frederick, long-time friend of the artist, has assembled outstanding examples of Graves's work over the years.

Contemporary with these are water colors in which Graves is on more familiar ground; birds drawn in ink on paper with a Chinese brush, the art—the capture of some component of personality—managed by gesture. But the gesture is a composite, half in the object drawn, half in the legible skill of hand. Here again, Graves is intent on his new major key, effected largely with the use of gold backgrounds. The paintings ask a little more distance of the onlooker. Several Spirit Birds, and the TROUT IN STREAM of the Mr. and Mrs. Lawrence Fleischman Collection fall into this luminous pattern.

For all the justifications, Graves was uneasy in his new house, viewed it as a work of art to be completed, was freedom-and-journey conscious—detaching himself. In the autumn of 1954 he went to Japan, for the specific purpose of learning how to mount paper on frames on a larger scale. "To make screens out of more than one piece, to avoid too much wrinkling of paper so that it gets in the way." He has at present an expert mounter, but Graves wants to be independent.

After Japan, Graves went to Ireland, where he has lived these last two winters in County Cork. He lives on an island in a river. He was in search of a Northwest climate somewhere else in the world. Ireland was a deliberate choice—not without an element of risk, for the elusive lies in wait for you there. A sense of artistry, a sort of low-grade fever, is as pervasive as the humidity, and the artist's feeling for the duplicity of existence is taken for granted. What is harder come by is discipline. To crystallize something in Ireland is a difficult matter.

But this is seeing the country as a land of people. Graves inhabits as well a more universal world of living things. In Ireland he has come up with drawings of hedgerow creatures. The weasel or ferret has lent itself well to Graves's understanding of impulse; so has the fox, balled up against the winter in its

54

Spirit Bird, No. 6, 1953
Mrs. Donald E. Frederick, Seattle

Trout in Stream, 1953
Mr. and Mrs. Lawrence Fleischman, Detroit

hole. A zone of climate is to such creatures what nationality is to us. Graves leaves the Northwest "to possess his own life," in other words, to possess his own past in useful detachment. "I have memorized the Northwest so I can use it. When I am away I can use it as much as I wish. It does not crowd me like a new environment. I have it in memory."

The few oils from Ireland, still more recent than the drawings, are most distinguished when they are most abstract. FLIGHT OF PLOVER is the finest and purest Graves: a fluid pattern of living motion, in the control of that instinct which makes a spiritual harmony out of many living things.

To come to the heart of the matter, Graves gives us an image or a symbol loose and aloof in a void which has yet to be disciplined into time and space. This symbol exists in some antithetical contrast within itself, as between minnow and bird or fish and star, and the essential relationship, which carries the tension of the work, is between the symbol and *ourselves*. We become part, and the image adds to our definition. The artist does not mirror us, but he gives us an opportunity not to miss ourselves, and in this sense Graves is a religious artist. Hence the extraordinary hold upon us which his paintings possess.

FLIGHT OF PLOVER, 1955
The Whitney Museum of American Art, New York

CHRONOLOGY

1910 August 28: born Fox Valley, Oregon.

1910–1929 Lived Puget Sound region. Public school through second year high school.

1928 Summer: seaman, American Mail Line. One trip to Orient. Saw Tokyo and environs, Shanghai, Hong Kong, Philippines, Hawaiian Islands.

1929–1930 Lived with parents in Seattle for two more months of high school, then sailed as cadet on American Mail Line. Two trips to Orient.

1931 Returned in autumn. Left for Los Angeles with New Orleans as destination. Stayed in Los Angeles.

1932 Stopped to see aunt in Beaumont, Texas; finished high school in Beaumont. Three summer months in New Orleans. Returned home.

1933 Early oils in heavy paint. MOOR SWAN won $100 prize in Northwest Annual at Seattle Art Museum (October).

1934 Seattle: converted stable to studio with Guy Anderson. Began building studio in Edmonds on family property. Spring–summer: six months' trip from Seattle to Los Angeles with Guy Anderson. Stayed in Los Angeles.

1935 Left Los Angeles in February on news of father's death. Returned to Seattle. Summer: Sunflower Series.

1936 Worked for Federal Art Project. Summer: Red Calf Series painted in Puyallup Valley, south of Seattle.

1937 Painted Message Series for Federal Art Project.

1938–1939 Summer: settled in town of La Conner, north of Seattle. Produced Nightfall Pieces, as satire on Munich Conference. Autumn: Puerto Rico via New York. Visited galleries and Museum of Modern Art in New York. At San Juan, Puerto Rico, through March, 1939. Painted Purification Series. Home by April. Painted "falling chalices and compotes"; worked in tempera and wax. Association with Mark Tobey. Winter: Seattle. Four works for Federal Art Project exhibited at Museum of Modern Art. Paintings of Moons, Snake and Moon, Chalices date from this period.

1940 Spring: built on Fidalgo, one of San Juan Islands in Puget Sound, nearest to La Conner. Shack on precipitous site (named The Rock). September: on staff of Seattle Art Museum, full time until Christmas, but continued to be attached to museum until 1942.

1941 Painted Inner Eye Series. Graves's new work seen in Seattle by Dorothy C. Miller of the Museum of Modern Art.

1942	Shown in *Americans 1942*, Museum of Modern Art. Inducted into Army.
1943	Discharged from Army in April, and returned to The Rock where he expanded original shack into camp. Painted Joyous Young Pine Series, Journey Series.
1944	Painted Old Pine Top Series, Leaf Series.
1945	Crane Series. San Francisco: met Mischa Dolnicoff; further interest in Zen philosophy.
1946–1947	Awarded Guggenheim Fellowship for study in Japan: traveled as far as Honolulu, but military permit for civilian to enter Japan withheld. Met Japanese painter Yone Arashiro, in Honolulu. Painted Chinese Bronze Series

there (February to July). On return, moved away from The Rock and began building new home in Edmonds with help of Arashiro.

1948–1949	Summer: trip to Europe on invitation of collector Edward James. Paris, England, winter in Chartres, brief trip to Italy before returning to Edmonds in spring. Destroyed paintings from Chartres. Painted Bouquet Series.
1950	Six months' trip to Mexico.
1952–1953	Returned to large oils: YOUNG GANDER READY FOR FLIGHT, etc. Increased use of gold grounds.
1954–1956	Summer: completed building at Edmonds. Autumn: trip to Japan, then to County Cork, Ireland, where he has lived for last two years.

HIBERNATING ANIMAL, 1954
The Willard Gallery, New York

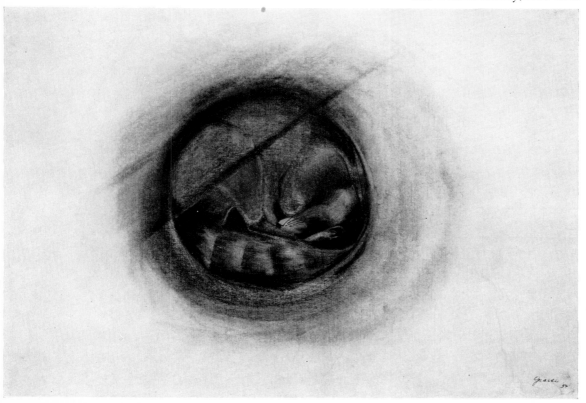

AWARDS

First Purchase Prize, Seattle Art Museum Annual Northwest Exhibition: 1933

John Simon Guggenheim Memorial Foundation Fellowship: 1946

Norman Wait Harris Medal, Art Institute of Chicago: 1947

Watson F. Blair Prize, Art Institute of Chicago: 1948

University of Illinois Purchase Prize: 1955

EXHIBITIONS

(One-man shows unless otherwise noted)

Seattle Art Museum: 1936

Museum of Modern Art, New York: Americans 1942—18 Americans from 9 States (31 items); Romantic Painting in America (4 items), 1943

Willard Gallery, New York: 1942, 1944, 1945, 1948, 1953, 1954

Arts Club of Chicago: 1943

University Gallery, Minneapolis: 1943

Detroit Institute of Arts: 1943

Phillips Gallery, Washington, D.C.: One of Three Loan Exhibitions (19 items), 1943; 1954

Philadelphia Art Alliance: 1946

California Palace of the Legion of Honor, San Francisco: Retrospective, 1948

Santa Barbara Museum of Art, Santa Barbara, California: 1948

Los Angeles County Museum: 1948

Art Institute of Chicago: Annual American Exhibition, Water Colors and Drawings (17 items), 1948

Margaret Brown Gallery, Boston: 1950

Mayo Hill Galleries, Wellfleet, Massachusetts: Morris Graves (12 items), Gyorgy Kepes, Mark Tobey, 1952

Beaumont Art Museum, Beaumont, Texas: 1952

Oslo Kunstforening, Oslo, Norway: 1955

WORKS IN PUBLIC COLLECTIONS

The Albright Art Gallery, Buffalo

The Art Gallery of Toronto

The Art Institute of Chicago

The Arts Club of Chicago

The Baltimore Museum of Art

The Cleveland Museum of Art

The Delaware Art Center, Wilmington, Delaware

The Detroit Institute of Arts

The Fogg Art Museum, Cambridge, Massachusetts

The Fort Wayne Art School and Museum

The Metropolitan Museum of Art, New York

The Milwaukee Art Institute

The Museum of Fine Arts, Boston

The Museum of Modern Art, New York

The Pasadena Art Museum, Pasadena, California

The Phillips Gallery, Washington, D.C.

The Portland Art Museum, Portland, Oregon

The San Francisco Museum of Art

The Seattle Art Museum

The University of Illinois Art Collection, Champaign-Urbana

The University of Nebraska Art Galleries, Lincoln

The Wadsworth Atheneum, Hartford

The Whitney Museum of American Art, New York

The Worcester Art Museum

SELECTED BIBLIOGRAPHY

BOOKS

Barr, Alfred H., Jr. *What Is Modern Painting?* 5th ed. rev. New York: Museum of Modern Art, 1952. Pp. 34, 35.

Baur, John I. H. *Revolution and Tradition in Modern American Art.* Cambridge: Harvard University Press, 1951. Pp. 118–119, 120, 133, 143.

Flexner, James T. *The Pocket History of American Painting.* New York: Pocket Books, 1950. Pp. 107–108, 115.

Frost, Rosamund. *Contemporary Art; the March of Art from Cézanne until Now.* New York: Crown Publishers, 1942. Pp. 31, 201, 219.

Janis, Sidney. *Abstract and Surrealist Art in America.* New York: Reynal & Hitchcock, 1944. Pp. 87, 91.

Myers, Bernard S. *Modern Art in the Making.* New York: Whittlesey House, 1950. Pp. 404, 405, 428.

Soby, James Thrall. *Contemporary Painters.* New York: Museum of Modern Art, 1948. Pp. 40–50.

Wight, Frederick S. *Milestones of American Painting in Our Century.* Boston: Institute of Contemporary Art; New York: Chanticleer Press, 1949. Pp. 24, 32, 108.

EXHIBITION CATALOGUES

Arts Club of Chicago. *Morris Graves.* Chicago, 1943.

California Palace of the Legion of Honor. *Morris Graves: Retrospective Exhibition.* San Francisco, 1948.

Mayo Hill Galleries, Inc. *Morris Graves, Gyorgy Kepes, Mark Tobey,* with introduction by Frederick S. Wight. Wellfleet, Massachusetts, 1952.

Museum of Modern Art. *Americans 1942. 18 Artists from 9 States,* edited by Dorothy C. Miller with statements by the artists. New York, 1942. Pp. 51–59, 124–125.

———. *Romantic Painting in America,* by James Thrall Soby and Dorothy C. Miller. New York, 1943. Pp. 48, 126, 135.

Phillips Memorial Gallery. *Cross Section Number One of a Series of Specially Invited American Paintings & Water Colors with Rooms of Recent Work by Max Weber, Karl Knaths, Morris Graves.* Washington, D.C., 1942.

———. *Three Loan Exhibitions: Recent Paintings in Gouache by Morris Graves, Paintings, Sculpture & Mobiles by Max Schallinger, Paintings by Artists of Washington, Baltimore and Vicinity,* with introduction by Duncan Phillips. Washington, D.C., 1943.

Tate Gallery. *American Painting from the Eighteenth Century to the Present Day.* London, 1946. P. 13.

University of Minnesota Gallery. *40 American Painters.* Minneapolis, 1951.

Wadsworth Atheneum. *Seven by Six: Loan Exhibition of Contemporary Water Colors.* Hartford, 1948.

Willard Gallery. *Morris Graves, Exhibition of Recent Work,* with almost total reprint of introduction to *Three Loan Exhibitions* of 1943 written by Duncan Phillips. New York, 1944.

———. *Morris Graves,* with preface taken from *Elements of Buddhist Iconography* by Ananda K. Coomaraswamy and an extensive text by the artist. New York, 1948.

61

ARTICLES

Breuning, Margaret. "Avian Graves," *Art Digest,* November 15, 1948, p. 29.

Brian, Doris. "Fresh Wine in New Bottles, 1942 Vintage," *Art News,* February 1, 1942, p. 22.

Crowninshield, Frank. "Talent Scouts for Art," *Vogue,* May 15, 1942, pp. 55, 95.

Fitzsimmons, James. "Graves' Aviary of the Inner Eye," *Art Digest,* December 1, 1953, pp. 14, 31.

Greenberg, Clement. "Art," *The Nation,* February 17, 1945, p. 193.

Louchheim, Aline B. "Graves' New World," *Art News,* February 15, 1945, p. 18.

Millier, Arthur. "Laughton, Art Lover," *Art Digest,* February 15, 1949, pp. 9–10.

Phillips, Duncan. "Morris Graves," *Magazine of Art,* December 1947, pp. 305–308.

Rexroth, Kenneth. "The Visionary Painting of Morris Graves," *Perspectives USA,* Winter 1955, pp. 58–66.

Soby, James Thrall. "The Younger American Artists," *Harper's Bazaar,* April 1944, pp. 77, 162.

Sutton, Denys. "The Challenge of American Art," *Horizon,* October 1949, p. 283.

Sweeney, James Johnson. "Five American Painters," *Harper's Bazaar,* April 1944, pp. 77, 162.

Sweet, Frederick A. "Morris Graves and Lyonel Feininger," *Bulletin of the Art Institute of Chicago,* September 15, 1948, pp. 65–67.

Tannenbaum, Libby. "Notes at Mid-Century," *Magazine of Art,* December 1950, pp. 291, 292.

Valentiner, William R. "Morris Graves," *Art Quarterly,* December 1944, pp. 250–256.

Wilenski, Reginald H. "A London Look at U.S. Painting in the Tate Gallery Show," *Art News,* August 1946, p. 24.

ANIMAL, No. 1, 1954
The Willard Gallery, New York

PAINTINGS AND DRAWINGS